First published in France in 1993 by Société Nouvelle des Editions du Chêne
Published in France in 2000 by Editions du Chêne-Hachette Livre
First published in the UK in 2000 by Cassell & Co

This edition first published in 2006 by Cassell Illustrated
a division of Octopus Publishing Group Ltd
2–4 Heron Quays, London E14 4JP

A CIP catalogue record for this book is available from the British Library

ISBN-13: 978-1-844035-41-0
ISBN-10: 1-844035-41-7
10 9 8 7 6 5 4 3 2 1

Design: François Huertas
Editors: Claire Cornubert and Joan Le Boru
English Editor: Lisa Davidson
English Translator: Sally Laruelle

CATS

Yann Arthus-Bertrand

TEXT BY: Danièle Laruelle
CONSULTANT: Sabine Paquin
International feline judge
PHOTOGRAPHS BY: Yann Arthus-Bertrand

ONCE THERE WALKED ... THE CAT

"I am not a friend, and I am not a servant. I am the Cat who walks by himself,
and I wish to come into your Cave."

This is how the cat in a Rudyard Kipling story addresses the woman who has used her magic powers to enslave some of the wild beasts of the forest – the dog, the horse and the cow. The cat has taken care not to be bewitched: it comes of its own accord to claim its rightful place by the fireside, and charms the woman by playing with the baby and devouring the dreaded mouse. This apparently innocent children's story in fact captures both the real and mythical essence of the cat. The playful little pet with its gentle purr reverts into a dangerous predator as soon as it's let loose, and even if well fed, behaves like a sadistic killer. It is still "the cat who goes through the Wet Wild Woods, waving his wild tail and walking by his wild lone". Some have even suggested that it is the cat who tamed man – unless it actually tamed woman, as in Kipling's story.

Indeed, throughout the ages, from one culture to another, the cat has always been associated with femininity. As Kipling knew, and as the snake in the garden of Eden taught us, it's a short step from woman to devil: the cave woman in his story is a kind witch, and the cat a worthy descendant of Lucifer, the angel of light whose pride led to his fall. Because of these dubious connections, the poor cat has undergone many trials and tribulations in the Western world. Felis catus was sanctified, deified and embalmed in the Egypt of the Pharaohs; considered protector of home and childhood in the Gallo-Roman era; then in the Middle Ages condemned to be burned at the stake, ritually sacrificed or simply tortured! This sad state of affairs persisted in certain places until the early nineteenth

PRECEDING DOUBLE PAGE AND LEFT: Bengal's Hill's Hearty, Snow Chocolate Spotted Tabby Bengal, belonging to Mr. and Mrs. Michel Sfez-Zon.

century, but could not stop the irresistible ascension of Master Cat: mouse hunter and rat killer extraordinaire, he protected lofts and granaries, and helped keep the plague at bay; his decorative grace soon won him a place in drawing rooms, and the admiration of the powerful, such as French statesman Cardinal de Richelieu, who caused quite a stir by bequeathing part of his fortune to his fourteen cats! The cat padded on velvet paws into the literature of the sixteenth and seventeenth centuries, and was adopted by many Romantic writers for the very "darkness" which had been its downfall in the Middle Ages. It then became a favourite companion to many a poet, settling down among the stacks of books and papers, to watch over their writings much as it used to observe the strange spells of the alchemists.

The brief overview of the adventures of the cat in the Western world demonstrates the ambivalence of human feelings towards an animal which retains a certain mystery – as mankind generally mistrusts what it doesn't understand, we associate this mystery with black magic. The tiger in the London Zoo inspired the poet Paul Valéry to write two pages which come close to defining this elusive feline quality: "I fall into a reverie before this impenetrable animal being (…). In my innocence, I search its admirable muzzle for human

Sascha de Nydou, Russian Blue, belonging to Mr. and Mrs. Bernhard Mühlheim.

qualities. I am held in its grip by its expression of impassive superiority, of power and of absence (…). What completeness, what absolute egotism, what sovereign isolation! Its full potential is ever imminent. This creature leaves me dreaming of a vast empire."

Such reflections could also be applied to the cat, the tiny distant cousin of the Great King of the felines, but the qualities that make the tiger so gloriously imperial are merely misplaced pride and self-importance in the cat. It is too small for such lofty ambitions – at least in the eyes of humans, who, after all, tamed the horse and the dog.

In the early Middle Ages, when the Christian church sought to consolidate its conquests, the cat's empire was thought to be that of evil. This naturally Luciferian creature demonstrated its supreme wickedness with its noisy love-life and sensuality. No wonder, then that women were portrayed meeting their lovers at night or going to the devil's Sabbaths – veritable orgies – disguised as cats. When these "witches" were captured, they were burned along with some innocent cat. Other women were burned as heathens too, just because they took care of the handicapped, knew herbal recipes or had mysterious powers. And the cat, who befriended the poor and asked nothing in return, was always burned with them. The church asserted its power through these acts and made the cat its scapegoat, a symbol of wantonness and obscurantism.

Geisha de la Lumière Cendrée, Shaded Golden Persian,
belonging to Mr. and Mrs. Robert Bonnin.

The Age of Enlightenment heralded a brighter chapter in this dark and bloody history. At the court of Louis XV – who loved Persian cats – a certain François Augustin Paradis de Moncrif was the first to sing the praises of the feline race in his *History of Cats*, published in 1727. He was greatly ridiculed for this work, however, as the Age of Reason was still one of ambivalence: some ladies fainted at the sight of a cat, others cultivated their company, wrote verses to them and had tombs erected for them. In *Natural History*, written by French naturalist Georges Buffon some thirty years after Moncrif's text, there is a hateful portrait of the cat, totally lacking in scientific objectivity. Moncrif may have erred in his excessively romantic portrayal and some of his writings now seem ridiculous, but at least he demonstrated, with scholarly quotations, poems and proverbs, that the cat has always been part of society; it has always had enemies, but it has also always had influential supporters.

Historical records concentrate so much on persecution and on witches' trials that we guiltily begin to wonder how poor *Felis catus* survived the carnage at all. But history never mentions the affection of anonymous cat-lovers for a creature which, after all, was both useful ratter and pleasant companion.

The true history of the cat has yet to be written, and perhaps will always remain as

Hanske de la Cachouteba, Blue Tabby and White Norwegian Forest Cat, belonging to Mrs. Christine Pochez.

discreet as a feline's soft foot-steps on sand.

The cat is indifferent to its past and cares nothing for its future; it has nine lives, after all, and has thrived despite its woes. It has diversified too, thanks to secret admirers and breeders.

By the late nineteenth century, it had become so popular that the first cat shows were organized. Institutions were created to define the standards of the various breeds and to maintain them through selective breeding. The age of the champion cat had dawned – a feline aristocracy, which will be our guide throughout this book. Discover the cat in all its shapes and forms, its relationship to man, to time and place, its role in folklore and the arts, through these portraits of cats and portraits of cat-lovers; birds of a feather, after all! As for all the meanings of the word feline – dip into this book, and you'll see for yourself.

Filomène des Fauves et Or, Blue Somali, belonging to Mrs. Christine Le Renard.

SHORT-HAIRED CATS

KORAT

The Korat, from Thailand, is a medium-sized cat with a rounded back, creating an impression of power without heaviness. The tail and legs, ending in oval paws, must be proportionate to the body. The uniform blue-grey coat is fine and glossy, lying close to the body.

The tips of the fur give the coat its silver sheen. The muzzle and pads are a dark blue-grey or lavender colour. The head, viewed from the front, is heart-shaped, accentuated by the arched eyebrow ridges.

The nose is rounded just above the muzzle, and is neither too long nor too short, with a "stop" at the base of the forehead. The well-developed chin must be neither pinched nor pointed. The large ears are wide at the base, set high on the head and covered in short, tight fur. The round, wide-open eyes are preferably bright green, but may also be amber-coloured.

In 1959 an American breeder was given a pair of Korats from Thailand, and she imported other cats to begin a breeding programme in the West. Thanks to the pedigree, we can trace the origin of the various lines back to Thailand,

PRECEDING PAGE: Carragato Lassik, Gold Spotted California Spangled, belonging to Mrs. Tatti.

where this cat is considered to bring good luck. The Bangkok library has drawings and manuscripts about the Korat dating from 1350 to 1767. We can assume, therefore, that the breed has survived practically pure, even if the ancient descriptions seem fanciful and somewhat Asian in phrasing: "The fur of its coat has roots the colour of clouds, tips the colour of silver, and its eyes shine like dewdrops on a lotus leaf."

RIGHT AND PRECEDING PAGE: Ejalma d'Osiria de Passaya of Yun Agor, Fyindee de Yun Agor d'Orfeny and Grawal Ier de Yun Agor d'Orfeny, Korats, belonging to Mrs. Claudine Dotte.

RUSSIAN BLUE

The Russian Blue has a graceful, elongated body with slender legs and small oval paws. It is medium-sized, with an elegant neck and a long, tapering tail. Its double coat, with a silver sheen, distinguishes it from other Blues. Its fur is short, thick, very fine, and stands out slightly from the body, unlike the Korat's close-lying coat. The head is short and wedge-shaped. The nose and forehead are straight but there is a slight curve beginning at the level of the eyebrows. The ears are large and rather pointed, with such fine skin that they look transparent; they are scantily covered with fur inside.

This cat, with its beautiful bright green gaze, also differs from the Korat in that its eyes are almond-shaped. Round eyes are not acceptable in a Russian Blue, and neither is a massive or Siamese-type body. Otherwise known as "Archangel Blue", "Spanish Blue" or "Maltese", the Russian Blue was introduced into England in the mid-1800s by sailors returning from Russia, and, like many other cats, keeps its origins a close secret, but is thought to come from the northern regions.

During World War II, the breed nearly died out; in order to save it, breeders crossed it with British Blue and Siamese,

which was disastrous. Apart from the morphological changes, the resulting cats did not have the characteristic double coat.

During the 1960s concerted efforts were made to return to the original type and keep it. On a more worldly note, the breed boasts a famous aristocrat: the very noble Vashka, who was the companion of Nicholas I, czar of Russia from 1825 to 1855.

RIGHT AND PRECEDING PAGE: Sascha de Nydow and Saskia de Nydow, Russian Blues, belonging to Mr. and Mrs. Bernhard Mühlheim.

BRITISH SHORTHAIR

"We would do well to look to the gutters for our education," wrote Moncrif in his History of Cats in 1727. The nineteenth-century cat-lover and painter Harrison Weir must have agreed with him, as he hand-picked cats from the gutters of Great Britain to breed and show, thereby raising the common or garden alley cat to the rank of "British Shorthair". This terribly colonialist appellation was used at the time to refer to a variety of continental household cats, and was the cause of much confusion, until specific breeding programmes defined the precise standards for British and European Shorthairs, according to morphological differences.

Nowadays, the British Shorthair still has a slightly rugged look which betrays its common origins. It is a medium-sized cat, with a sturdy, muscular body, broad shoulders, short robust legs, and a deep, rounded chest. The tail is thick at the base, and should be as long as two-thirds of the body. The head must not be too short, and is round, like the muzzle. The eyes are also round, and are orange, gold or copper-coloured; in the case of silver-coated cats, the eyes should be green, and white cats can be odd-eyed.

The eyes are set quite wide apart, accentuating the width of the nose, and there is a very slight stop between the nose and the well-defined forehead. The very thick, short hair covering the forehead gives it a rounded look. The ears are quite wide at the base, and quite small, with rounded tips. Its short, plush fur makes this cat look round and fluffy – most inviting to the touch! With its sweetly innocent, picture-book face, it looks just like a cuddly toy come to life.

RIGHT AND PRECEDING PAGE: Vincent van Lady's Home, Whoopy van Lady's Home and Grisella van Kievietsdel, British Blue Shorthairs, belonging to Mrs. Els H. Franssen van der Meer.

ABOVE AND RIGHT: Avram Van Diaspora, Lilac British Shorthair,
belonging to Mrs. Béatrice Passin.

Above: Gimini Silver du Rio d'Erclin, Silver Classic Tabby British Shorthair, belonging to Mr. and Mrs. Georges Vallez.
Right: Aldo de la Chezine, Cream British Shorthair, belonging to Mr. and Mrs. André Martaud.

SELKIRK REX

Hello, I'm the Selkirk Rex. My nickname is the "Sheepcat",
though I'm named after a breed of rabbit (and sometimes
I hop, too)! My curly coat is a rarity that I share with the little
long-eared herbivore, and with my cousins from Devon and
Cornwall, but otherwise we look quite different.

My English cousins and I also have our humble origins
in common: we were discovered in litters of ordinary kittens,
after a natural mutation. The breeders thought we were so
pretty they decided to establish our breed.

*RIGHT AND FOLLOWING DOUBLE PAGE: Halvane du Parc, White Selkirk Rex,
belonging to Mr. and Mrs. Jacques Courdille.*

I am the youngest Rex to date; my ancestor, Miss Pesto, was born in Wyoming in 1987, of a common American mother and unknown father. She was adopted by Mrs. Newman, a Montana breeder of Persian cats, and moved up into high society!

Her first partner, a black Persian called Photo Finish, gave her three curly kittens, so the Selkirk is genetically dominant, because just one Selkirk parent was enough to produce these curly little cats. I'm very proud of my ancestors – I owe them my robust, gracefully rounded body – but I'm even prouder of my three kinds of curly hair, and of my eyebrows and whiskers!

Above and following double pages: Happy-Jolly du Parc,
Solid Red Selkirk Rex, belonging to Mr. and Mrs. Jacques Courdille.

DEVON REX

The Devon Rex is a slender cat with a firm, muscular body, long, slim legs, and a tapering, pointed tail. Its long, elegant neck carries a wedge-shaped head with high cheekbones, a strong chin, a short, pinched muzzle and a short nose. Its forehead curves back to a flat skull. Its wide-based ears are huge and low-set, giving the cat its impish air. Its large, oval eyes are set on a slight slant. Finally, like all the Rex cats, the Devon Rex has a curly coat.

The first Rex of this kind was discovered in 1960 in an abandoned tin mine in Devon. It mated with a tortie-and-white female stray, and one of the resulting male kittens had its father's curly coat. This kitten was named "Kirlee" by its adoptive owner: mating was attempted with the Cornish Rex, but the resulting litters were hopelessly straight-haired, and an inbreeding programme was therefore used to establish the breed.

Honesty Van Zechique, Tortie Tabby Devon Rex, belonging to Mrs. Marijke Wijers.

Above, right and following double page: Jewel Tiffany Van Zechique, Red Shaded Cameo Devon Rex, belonging to Mrs. Marijke Wijers.

Above: Honey Bee Van Zechique, White Devon Rex.
right: Jewek Tiffany Van Zechique, Red Shaded Cameo Devon Rex, both belonging to Mrs. Marijke Wijers.

CORNISH REX

The Cornish Rex was the first of all Rex cats, appearing on July 21, 1950. It was a curly little mutant in a litter of ordinary kittens whose mother, Serena, was an unexceptional farm cat. Serena's owner, a breeder of curly-coated Rex rabbits, was charmed by this strange kitten. She was advised to mate it back to its mother to obtain other curly offspring. Two years later, Serena produced an ordinary female kitten and two curly-coated males. This new breed took a while to establish, because one of the kittens disappeared, and the other one was rendered sterile when it was adult. Fortunately, it already had descendants, and the mutant gene was preserved by crossing with Burmese and British Shorthair, which resulted in a diversification of colours, and helped establish a type and avoid inbreeding.

The new cat was called "Cornish" because it was born in Cornwall, and "Rex" … because of the rabbit. The Cornish Rex has a short, dense, curly or wavy coat.

Unlike the Devon Rex, it has no guard hairs at all. It has long, crinkled whiskers and eyebrows. It is slimmer than the Devon Rex, with a medium-sized, very muscular body.

Carlozio's Raphael Gold, Devon Rex Chocolate Tonkinois,
belonging to Mrs. Anna Maria Quintela.

With its long, slender legs and long, tapering tail, it has all the elegance of a feline greyhound, a characteristic which American breeders have accentuated by crossing it with Siamese and Orientals.

Seen in profile, the head is flat at the top, then curves gently at the forehead, and continues in a straight line to the tip of the nose. The eyes are oval, wide-open and slightly slanting. They may be any colour, but must be in keeping with the coat. The large ears are wide at the base and slightly rounded at the tips, but, unlike those of the Devon Rex, they are set high on the head and are more conical in shape. They are covered in very fine hair, but do not have the tufts which adorn the tips of the Devon's ears.

RIGHT: Héloïse de Cléomont, Smoky Black and White Cornish Rex,
belonging to Mr. Jean-Pierre Filippi.
FOLLOWING DOUBLE PAGE: Honey Bee Van Zechique, White Devon Rex,
belonging to Mrs. Marijke Wijers.

Gaston (ABOVE AND RIGHT), Framboise du Pen Cuckoo and Hela d'Aba,
Cornish Rex, belonging to Mr. and Mrs. Laurent Maillet.

EUROPEAN SHORTHAIR

And here it is, the cat that is loved just for itself, the gentle household pet, the everyday cat, the town cat and the country cat, the ordinary cat in all its glory: the European. Although it arrived in Gaul with the Roman armies, it was not recognized as a distinct breed in cat shows until 1983! Yet it has made a significant contribution to folklore and literature, has been of great service and has paid a high price, especially to skin-merchants and witch-burners.

How could European cat-lovers ignore it, when it stands on every street corner, scoffing at the breeds of greater renown with their more exotic origins? Its very ordinariness has become its distinguishing feature: the European is an average cat, ideally resembling the common household cat, and its main quality is that it lacks the qualities of the other breeds!

The European must not have an elongated body like a Siamese or Oriental, nor a "chunky" body like the British or the Exotic Shorthair. It can be from medium-sized to large, and is sturdy, supple and muscular with thick, strong legs proportionate to its body, and a broad, deep chest. Its head is quite big and rounded, but otherwise there is nothing

Glaçon, White European, belonging to Mrs. Monique Barbotte.

"round" in this cat's appearance. Its nose is straight, and of the same width all down its length. The base of its forehead is well-defined, but the European does not have a stop – unlike its British cousin, which also has smaller ears. Its round eyes are set well apart at a slight slant, and they can be green, yellow or orange. White cats can have blue eyes, or eyes of different colours. Its fur is short, thick and glossy, with neither the smooth sheen of an Oriental nor the downiness of an American. In short, the European is extraordinarily average!

RIGHT AND FOLLOWING DOUBLE PAGE: Danube, Blue Spotted European, belonging to Mrs. Daniela Goll.

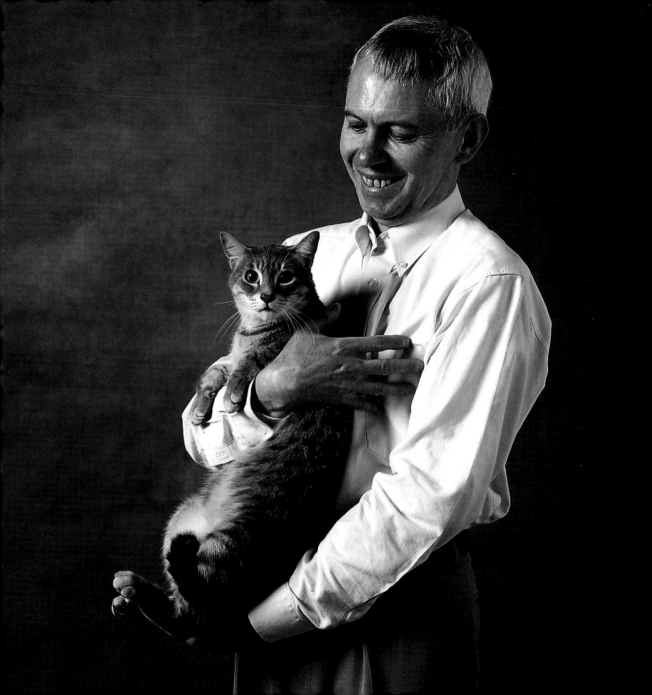

*Above: Zazie, Black and White European,belonging to
Mr. Claude Paul and Mr. Marcel Godenir.
Right: Fugue du Val aux Biches, Brown Classic Tabby
European, belonging to Mrs. Jacqueline Monnet.*

ABOVE: Glaçon, White European, belonging to Mrs. Monique Barbotte.
RIGHT AND FOLLOWING DOUBLE PAGE: Élodie des Mézières,
Golden Classic Tabby European, and her kittens, belonging to
Ms. Suzanne Piqué.

SPHYNX

No, I'm not a four-legged bat, or a medieval gargoyle come
to life … Don't you like me? Do you find my nakedness
indecent? Come, come, am I any more naked than you?
You want to know where I come from? Well I shan't tell
you … because I am a sphynx, after all, so I ask the questions!
Wouldn't you like to stroke my soft skin? It would be a
change from fur! But maybe you don't like my wrinkles.

    I'm actually a kind of Devon Rex, minus the fur …
which makes me all the more of a mutant. In any case, those
Rex cats are just beginners at the mutation game, but I'm an
old-timer! I have ancestors on pre-Colombian engravings;
scientists spotted me in 1830 in Paraguay and in 1900 in
Mexico – and now that I'm being seriously bred, you'll just
have to put up with me!

*RIGHT AND FOLLOWING DOUBLE PAGES: Phalaenopsis Georgette à Poil!, Brown
Tortie Tabby and White Sphynx, belonging to Mr. Patrick Challain and Mr. Guy
André Pantigny.*

JAPANESE BOBTAIL

The Japanese Bobtail is svelte and muscular, with a rounded muzzle and a triangular head; it owes its name to its short pom-pom tail. Its high cheekbones and slanting eyes seem to confirm its Asian origins, which go back to the seventh century. When standing, its longer hind legs are bent; when sitting, it often raises one of its forepaws, a gesture which is immortalized in many Japanese statuettes called "Maneki-neko" (Beckoning Cats). They are supposed to bring wealth when their left paw is raised, happiness when it's the right one … and when the living animal is tri-coloured, it keeps evil spirits at bay!

Izumo von der Baderstadt, Japanese Bobtail, belonging to Mr. Rolf Voehringer.

Passetis Chase (ABOVE) and Ioko-Omo von der Baderstadt (RIGHT),
Japanese Bobtails, belonging to Mr. Rolf Voehringer.

AMERICAN SHORTHAIR

The cat pictured here is an American Shorthair, an immigrant that headed West with the pioneers. Its body shape is very similar to that of its European cousins, but it has a rougher coat – a reminder of its adventurous life no doubt – and of course it's bigger, like all things American!

ABOVE, LEFT AND FOLLOWING DOUBLE PAGE: Miribu's Bustopher Jones of Phalaenopsis, Brown Classic Tabby American Shorthair, belonging to Mr. Guy-André Pantigny.

AMERICAN CURL

As for us, we are the curly-eared "American Curl" – we appeared after a chance mutation in the early 1980s.

As we're so new, our type is not quite fixed yet, apart from our ears, which are wide at the base and curl up, ideally in smooth arcs. Our fur can be short, dense and close-lying, or semi-long, smooth and silky, without an undercoat or ruff.

What else? Well, we're medium-sized, with a more or less elongated body. Our head is longer than it is wide; we have a straight nose, without a stop, and a gently curving forehead. Our large, oval eyes are set well apart, and they correspond with our coat, which can be any colour.

RIGHT AND FOLLOWING DOUBLE PAGE: Hollywood Chewing Gum de Cour Saint-Éloi, Red and White American Curl, belonging to Ms. Florence Prescott.

ABOVE AND LEFT: Harmonie d'un soir des Fleurs du Mal, American Curl, belonging to Mr. Christian Doublet.

ABOVE AND RIGHT: Free Taxe de Cour St Éloi, Tortie Smoke American Curl,
belonging to Ms. Florence Prescott.

BURMESE

The elegant figure of the Burmese distinguishes it both from the slimmer Oriental and the heavier European. It has a medium-sized, vigorous, muscular body, with a strong, rounded chest and a perfectly straight back. Its legs are relatively slender and well-proportioned, with small round paws. Its head is rounded, tapering to a short triangle. It has full cheeks (especially the male). The medium-sized ears are broad at the base, set well apart and tilting slightly forward. There is a break between nose and forehead. The muzzle must not be pinched, and is characterized by a strong lower jaw and well-developed chin. The lower line of the eyes should be rounded, but the upper line slants towards the nose. Eye colours may vary from yellow to amber, with a preference for gold. The fur is short, fine, very glossy and satin-like, with practically no undercoat. The coat should have no marks or stripes, but certain coat colours gradually lighten toward the sides and belly.

The Burmese have their origins in a cat called "Wong Mau", brought back from Rangoon to the U.S.A. in 1930. At first it was crossed with a seal point Siamese called "Tai Mau", and produced some Siamese-type kittens and others

RIGHT: Houdette de Treuzy known as Élisa, Chocolate Burmese, belonging to Mr. Sébastien Bonutti.

that looked like their mother. By mating the non-Siamese kittens with each other and with their mother, the Burmese breed was fixed, and was officially recognized in America in 1936.

Registration had to be suspended in the 1940s, however, as the importance of the Siamese line was threatening to eliminate the characteristics of the original breed. The American breeders got back to work on the selection process; meanwhile, the English, who had imported Burmese in 1947, were developing their own breeding programme, and recognized the breed officially in 1952. The following year, the American Burmese was registered again, this time for good. Today, the American type can be distinguished from the British by its more robust, less oriental morphology.

Kittens of Eesara Cha Iro No Ran, Sable Burmese,
belonging to Mrs. Béatrice Wood.

TONKINESE

The Tonkinese has only the most distant connection with
the Orient, as the breed was in fact developed in America,
a cross between a Burmese and a Siamese. It was recognized
in Canada in 1974, and in the United States in the 1980s,
but has yet to be officially registered in Europe – although
it is recognized by independent clubs. It is the perfect
synthesis of its parents – more svelte than the Burmese, but
heavier than the elongated Siamese. Its colour is like that of
the Burmese, but it has dark Siamese points. Its head is not
as round as that of the Burmese, nor as triangular as that of
present-day Siamese. It has aquamarine or pale turquoise eyes.

This genetic hybrid should please those who are nostalgic
for past aesthetic standards, like those of the first English
Burmese and the early, more rounded Siamese.

Hug Cha Iro No Ran, known as Duchesse, Natural Mink Tonkinese,
belonging to Mrs. Jocelyne Majus.

Left: Thamakan Silver Jeannet, Silver Burmilla, belonging to
Mrs. Anna Maria Quintela.
Above: One of Eesara Cha Iro No Ran's kittens, Sable Burmese,
belonging to Mrs. Béatrice Wood.

BURMILLA

Like the Tonkinese, the Burmilla is part Burmese, but it was not developed as a result of breeders' efforts. In fact it was the accidental fruit of an "unscheduled" love affair – between a female lilac Burmese and a male Chinchilla Persian, both belonging to Baroness Miranda von Kirchberg. As the owners of "quality" cats attach great importance to the purity of the breed, one can imagine that the lady in question was hardly overjoyed to learn of this illegitimate affair! But when the fraudulent kittens were born in Great Britain in 1981, they were so cute that they made up for their parents' wicked ways, and became the founders of an authentic new breed.

The Burmilla resembles the Burmese in its elegant shape, slender legs, slanting eyes and the general appearance of its head. It has the Chinchilla's dark pencilling on its cheeks and around its eyes – which are always a beautiful green – and the characteristic tipping which gives the coat its highlights. Its fur is thick and close-lying, longer than that of the Burmese. The coloured tips of its hairs can be all the Burmese colours (sable, chocolate, blue, lilac, red, cream) or black like the Chinchilla on a golden or silver undercoat.

RIGHT AND FOLLOWING DOUBLE PAGE: Thamakan Silver Jeannet, Silver Burmilla, belonging to Mrs. Anna Maria Quintela, photographed with Mrs. Marianne Paquin.

BOMBAY

The Bombay, a cross between a sable Burmese and a black
American Shorthair, is a relatively recent breed. Its glossy fur
is short, close-lying, and must be jet-black to the roots, like its
skin, nose and pads. Its round eyes are set far apart, and range
in colour from gold to copper – no other colours are allowed.
The head and muzzle are rounded, it has full cheeks, and
medium-sized, broad-based ears which tilt slightly forwards,
like those of the Burmese. Its nose is fairly short, with a slight
stop between the eyes. This breed was recognized in America
in 1976 and is now fixed, but crossings are still allowed
between Bombay and Burmese. It's a mini-panther, which
owes its exotic name to its dangerous, Indian cousin … but
our little one is gentle and affectionate, as if to contradict the
many, age-old legends about the black cat and its wickedness.

RIGHT AND FOLLOWING DOUBLE PAGE: Fejuko's Jeanette Isabella, Bombay,
belonging to Mr. Michel Le Hir.

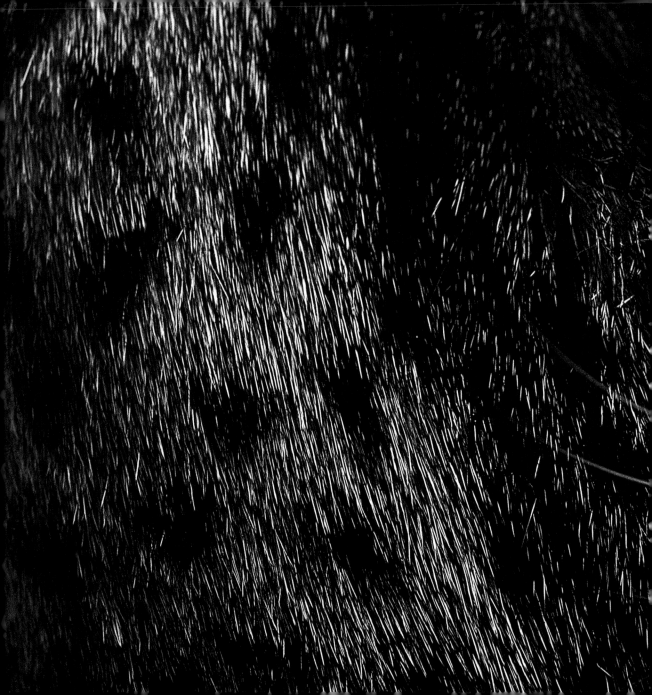

EGYPTIAN MAU

In Egypt, homeland of this breed with its finely spotted coat and distinctive gooseberry-coloured eyes, "Mau" means "cat". It is reminiscent of the Abyssinian with its strong, supple body, which must be neither heavy nor elongated.

It has a slightly rounded, wedge-shaped head, a short nose, and medium to large ears with furnishings inside. Its forehead is marked with an "M", and its almond-shaped eyes are elongated with fine lines. Its tail is marked with rings, and its neck with an open collar. Its hind legs have stripes, most of which do not form complete rings. Its fur is fine, silky and close-lying, with two bands of ticking. The first authentic Maus were introduced into Italy in the 1950s; they then accompanied their owner to the United States where the breed was recognized in 1978.

Meanwhile, British breeders, unable to import the cat because of quarantine regulations, tried to recreate it by crossing Abyssinians with various tabbies and Siamese. The result, which was disappointing in comparison with the original, became known as the Oriental Spotted Tabby.

RIGHT, PRECEDING DOUBLE PAGE AND FOLLOWING DOUBLE PAGES: Junglebook Aspen Mist, Silver Egyptian Mau, belonging to Mrs. Ingrid B. Baur-Schweizer.

BENGAL

The Bengal is a relatively recent breed, another product of civilized man's efforts to realize his dreams through the science of feline breeding. Man seems to be haunted by the fantasy of having a more or less tame, small-scale model of the terrible wild cats of the jungle in his living-room.

The Bengal is a result of this "Mowgli complex"; an American breeder developed it from a hybrid, produced by mating European or American Shorthairs with *Felis bengalensis*, an Asian wild cat also known as the "Leopard Cat". The first kittens were mated with Egyptian Maus and other spotted cats.

This hybridization programme, started in the 1960s, has produced a big, powerful, muscular cat with a strong bone structure, which looks rather like a wild animal. It has a squat neck and a rounded head which seems rather small in proportion to its body. The oval eyes are set well apart, and slightly slanting; the ears point slightly forwards.

The fur is short, thick and rather fluffy-looking, but soft and satiny to the touch. Dark spots cover the back, sides and belly; its head, shoulders and legs are striped, and its tail is ringed, with a dark tip.

RIGHT AND PAGES 118–119: Bengal's Hill's Hearty, Snow Chocolate Spotted Tabby Bengal, belonging to Mr. and Mrs. Michel Sfez-Zon.

ABOVE AND RIGHT: Bengal's Hill's Honey-Moon, Brown Spotted Tabby Bengal,
belonging to Mr. and Mrs. Michel Sfez-Zon.

At the present time it would seem that this beautiful creature is not always very sweet-tempered, so breeders are trying to mellow its character – which is perhaps a good idea, seeing that the males can weigh up to 17 or 18 kilos!

Bengal's Hill's Hearty, Snow Chocolate Spotted Tabby Bengal,
belonging to Mr. and Mrs. Michel Sfez-Zon.

SINGAPURA

The Singapura and the European Shorthair have their place of origin in common: the street. The Singapura is nicknamed the "Drain Cat" in Singapore, and is very common throughout South-East Asia. It is no doubt thanks to its unloved, underfed ancestors that it is so elegantly small: an adult female weighs no more than two kilos, and a male hardly three!

It was noticed in the mid-1970s by American breeders who took it home in their baggage to turn it into a show breed. So here it is, with its slightly triangular, rounded head, its large ears and its enormous green, yellow or hazel eyes. Dark lines are pencilled from the brows and outside corner of the eyes, and go down the sides of the nose from the inner corner of the eyes. Its body is svelte and muscular, with strong legs tapering to small, oval feet with dark pink pads.

Its ivory and bronze coat is very short, silky and close-lying, with ticking like that of the Abyssinian. There are not yet many of these ex-Asian gutter cats in America … but they are an even greater rarity in Europe.

RIGHT, PRECEDING AND FOLLOWING DOUBLE PAGES: H-Butterfly du Fort Canning, Brown Tabby Singapura, belonging to Mr. Gérard Prescott.

OCICAT

In the mid-1960s, American breeder Virginia Daly was working on a breeding programme crossing Abyssinians and Siamese. A Chocolate Point Siamese male and a hybrid female produced an unexpected, completely spotted cat, which was called "Ocicat" (Ocelot + cat). The newcomer became the object of a specific breeding programme designed to fix the breed and to have it recognized.

The Ocicat is elegant and powerful, neither too thin nor too heavy, and must look like a small, wild feline. Its head should be neither too triangular nor too round, with full cheeks and a well-developed chin. Its muzzle is quite long, well-defined but not pointed, and its nose has a slight stop. Its large, almond-shaped eyes are very wide apart and slightly slanting; they may be of any colour except blue. Its medium-sized ears are straight, and set well to the sides of the head. It has powerful legs and strong, oval feet. The tail is quite long and slightly tapering. The coat's ticking gives it its clearly-defined "eye-spots." The head is striped, and the tail ringed.

Gitane du Vieux Pont, Brown Tabby Ocicat, belonging to Mrs. Suzanne Arelli.

*ABOVE: Gitane du Vieux Pont, Ocicat Brown Tabby, belonging
to Mrs. Suzanne Arelli.
RIGHT AND FOLLOWING DOUBLE PAGES: Hocy du Vieux Pont,
Silver Spotted Chocolate Ocicat, belonging to Mr. Fabrice Calmes.*

CALIFORNIA SPANGLED

I'm the California Spangled Cat, a pure product of feline breeding techniques! I was first conceived by a Hollywood scriptwriter, Paul Casey, who wanted me to look like the spotted wild cats of Africa. In the 1970s, specialists got to work to create me, mating British and American Shorthairs with a Cairo street cat, a house-cat from Malaysia, and a few Siamese thrown in for good measure. Mother Nature may be good at mixing races, but she would have had a hard time getting that lot together! My neighbour on the right here, and on the following pages, is a genuine showbiz glamour puss.

PRECEDING DOUBLE PAGE AND RIGHT: *Carragato Lassik, Gold Spotted California Spangled, belonging to Mrs. Vanna Maria Tatti.*
FOLLOWING DOUBLE PAGE: *Tootsie, non-pedigree cat, belonging to Mr. and Mrs. William Weldens.*

LEFT: Tootsie, non-pedigree cat, belonging to Mr. and Mrs. William Weldens.
ABOVE: Tatleberry Tywysog, Brown Tabby and White Manx,
belonging to Mrs. Huguette Noebels.

MANX

The squat, rounded body of the Manx is accentuated by its distinguishing feature: its lack of tail! It is average-sized, muscular and compact (in technical terms, "cobby"). Its strong forelegs are shorter than its muscular hind legs, so its rump looks like that of a bear, or a rabbit… and some of these cats advance in leaps called "Manx Hops."

It has a rounded head, with a muzzle which is slightly longer than it is wide. It has prominent cheeks and a curved forehead. Its big, round eyes are set well apart, at a slight slant. Their colour corresponds with that of the coat, which is silky with a close, thick undercoat. Ideally, the Manx is "Rumpy", i.e., with a small, round rump and no tail at all. However, the gene responsible for this mutation is variable: certain cats, known as "Rumpy Risers", have up to three coccygeal vertebrae covered with a tuft of hair; others, called "Stumpies", have an embryo tail up to four inches long. Some kittens are born with an almost normal-length tail; they are known as "tailed Manx", and only used for reproduction.

RIGHT: Tatleberry Tywysog, Brown Tabby and White Manx, belonging to Mrs. Huguette Noebels.

The Manx Cat, from the Isle of Man in the Irish Sea, is one of the oldest breeds of domestic cat. It attracted the attention of British breeders in the early 1900s. Initially, cats that were born with too long a coat were rejected from the breeding program; in the 1960s, Americans began to take an interest in these scorned creatures, and used them to produce a new breed which they called "Cymric" (Welsh for "Wales"!).

Shen's Lady (FOLLOWING DOUBLE PAGE), Yuki and Winnie de la Gambade, Manx, belonging to Mrs. Huguette Noebels.

SCOTTISH FOLD

Like the Manx, the Scottish Fold on the next pages also has a double, which is called the "Highland Fold" because of its fur. You will find it described on page 188, together with the Cymric, in the "Long-hair" section.

ABOVE, LEFT AND FOLLOWING DOUBLE PAGE: Mar de Barret, known as Liberty, Black and White Scottish Van Fold and Scotland Yard, Black Silver Tabby and White Scottish Van Fold, belonging to Mrs. Yannick Prescott-Quefféléant.

CHARTREUX

The Chartreux was made famous by French author Colette. This cat is a uniform blue-grey. Its bright, deep yellow or copper-coloured eyes stand out from this dark background. It is a strong, heavily built cat, with a broad chest and medium-length, powerful legs. It is distinguished from other Blues by its broad, rounded head, which is wider at the base with well-developed jowls (especially in males). There is a narrow, flat space between the ears, which are set high on the head, accentuating its distinctive shape. The nose is broad and straight, without a stop. Another characteristic feature is its thick and glossy fur, with a slightly woolly undercoat. The coat must be even in tone, without any tipping. There must be no highlights or markings of any kind, and no hint of green in the eyes.

RIGHT AND FOLLOWING DOUBLE PAGE: Darling du Sacré Cœur, Chartreux, belonging to Mrs. Marie-Lucie Malenovic.

ABYSSINIAN

The first Abyssinian was brought back to Britain from Abyssinia (now Ethiopia) in 1868, by the members of a military expedition, who named the cat "Zula" after the port where they had arrived. The breed was fixed in Britain, where, in order to keep the distinctive features of the original (especially her "ticked" coat), she was mated with carefully chosen local shorthairs, as similar to her as possible. However, a photo of the original proves that she did not look much like her modern-day descendants.

In 1871 the Abyssinian was presented at the first cat show at the Crystal Palace in London. In 1889, the first Standard of Points for the breed was published, and in 1926, the Abyssinian Cat Club was formed in England. The following year, the breed appeared in France, in the shape of a certain British-born "Ras Tafari."

It soon became extremely popular, and breeding programmes were set up all over Europe and America, where today it is one of the most popular breeds, along with Siamese and Persians. It is true that the Abyssinian is an exceptionally elegant cat, reminiscent of an Egyptian divinity.

RIGHT AND FOLLOWING DOUBLE PAGES: Diamond Silver d'Altaïr of Cinnamon's, Sorrel Silver Abyssinian, belonging to Mr. Gilles Guillaumes.

Above: Diamond Silver d'Altaïr of Cinnamon's, Sorrel Silver Abyssinian,
belonging to Mr. Gilles Guillaumes.
Right: Cinnamon's Fersen, Sorrel Abyssinian, belonging to Mr. Franck Massé.

Hot Shot Lone Star, Fiona Lone Star, Hennessy Lone Star and
Shechinah Esprit d'Amour, Ruddy Abyssinians, belonging to Mrs. Daniela Goll.

Above: Diamond Silver d'Altaïr of Cinnamon's,
Sorrel Silver Abyssinian, belonging to Mr. Gilles Guillaumes.
Right: Gennetic's Black Silver d'Alyse de la Pagerie, Black
Silver Abyssinian, belonging to Mrs. Alyse Brisson.

Its body is medium-sized, supple and muscular, with a long, tapering tail. It has long, slim legs with visible tendons, and small oval feet. Its head is triangular, with gently rounded, harmonious contours. It has a firm chin, a medium-sized nose and quite large rounded ears, which are usually furnished on the inside. Its large, almond-shaped eyes are circled with a dark line. They must be set well apart, and pure gold, green or amber in colour. The coat is short, fine and close-lying, with the characteristic two or three dark bands of ticking, the tips being preferably dark. Whether the coat colour is ruddy, sorrel, blue, fawn or silver, there must be no markings on the chest, belly or legs. The nose leather, pads, and sometimes the tip of the tail must correspond to certain criteria, depending on the coat colour.

Helwétia de Fontanalbe, Fawn Abyssinian, belonging to
Mrs. Marie-Louise Giraud.

*Bahariya's Tefnout Blue Genes (ABOVE), Blue Abyssinian,
and Zazie, Bi-color European, belonging to Mr. Claude Paul
and Mr. Marcel Godenir.*

Cinnamon's Fersen, Sorrel Abyssinian, belonging to Mr. Franck Massé.

LONG-HAIRED CATS

SOMALI

The Somali is a long-haired version of the Abyssinian.
This natural mutant appeared in the 1930s, but was excluded
from breeding programmes for a long time because of its fur,
and it was not until the 1960s that American breeders took
an interest in it. Nowadays, it is universally recognized; it
conforms to the same standard as the Abyssinian, except for
the length of its coat – which forms breeches and a ruff, but
has the same ticking.

PRECEDING PAGE: *Pandapaws Eddie, Bi-coloured Seal Ragdoll,*
belonging to Mrs. Tatti.
RIGHT: *Lynn Lee's Secret Wishes, Ruddy Somalis, belonging to*
Mr. and Mrs. Alain Piette.

ABOVE: Lynn Lee's Secret Wishes belonging to Mr. and Mrs. Alain Piette.
RIGHT AND FOLLOWING DOUBLE PAGE: Hyacinth des Fauve et Or, Blue Somali,
belonging to Mrs. Christine Le Renard.

Helie-Tim du Bois Galant, known as Heliot, Sorrel Somali,
belonging to Mr. Patrick-Michael Reygner.

SCOTTISH CATS

Like the Manx and the Cymric, the Scottish and the Highland Fold Cat are the result of a spontaneous mutation. In their case, it took place in Scotland in the 1960s. They are the same in all respects except for the length of their fur. They are rather short-bodied cats, with a particularly rounded appearance: they have medium-length legs with round paws, a rounded chest and body, and a rounded head. With their folded ears and big round eyes, they look a bit like owls. It seems that the mutant gene responsible for these curious folded ears is also the cause of bone problems; so the Folds are regularly mated with other breeds, to keep them healthy… all round!

RIGHT: *Hidole des Sentiers Sauvages, Highland Fold, belonging to Mr. and Mrs. Christian Doublet-Picroyer.*
PRECEDING DOUBLE PAGES AND FOLLOWING: *H2O de Cour Saint-Éloi, Tortoiseshell Cymric, belonging to Ms. Florence Prescott.*

NORWEGIAN FOREST CAT (NORSK SKOGKATT)

The sturdy-looking Norsk is a big, powerfully built cat with a long body. Its muscular hind legs are slightly longer than its front legs, and it has big round paws with tufts between the toes. Its head forms an equilateral triangle, tipped with long, straight, wide-open ears, which are set high on the head and well-furnished with fur inside; ideally, they also have lynx-like tufts at the tips. The chin must be very firm, and the profile absolutely straight, with no trace of a stop at the base of the forehead. The large, slightly slanting eyes can be of any color, regardless of the colour of the coat, which can itself be any colour except chocolate and lilac, and have any markings except pointed patterns. The cat carries its long, bushy tail proudly aloft; when it is laid back along its body, it should reach to its neck. Its semi-long fur is double, with a woolly undercoat, and a long, smooth, water-resistant outer coat on its back and sides. In winter, the cat has a full shirt front, breeches and side whiskers; but after the annual moult, only the tail remains bushy.

RIGHT AND FOLLOWING DOUBLE PAGE: Naima's Yacinta, White Norwegian Forest Cat (Norsk Skogkatt), belonging to Mrs. Theres Ramseyer.

*Above: Naima's Yacinta, White Norwegian Forest Cat (Norsk Skogkatt),
belonging to Ms. Theres Ramseyer.
Right and following double page: Hanske de la Cachouteba, Blue Tabby
and White Norwegian Forest Cat (Norsk Skogkatt), belonging
to Mrs. Christine Pochez.*

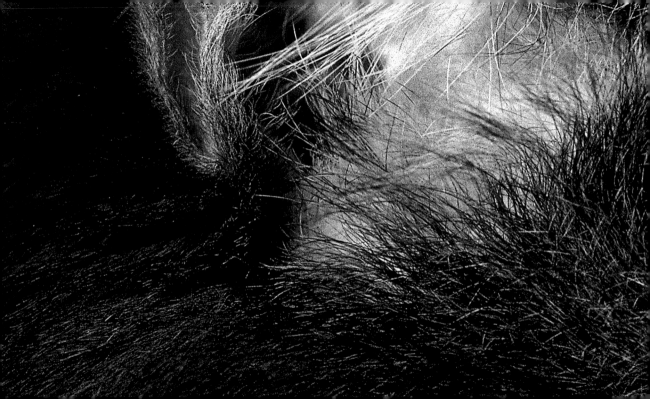

SIBERIAN FOREST CAT

In 1990, the Siberian Forest Cat came West, but it had already been bred in East Germany and Czechoslovakia for some years. Now that there is greater interest in the cat in Russia, a birth registry has been started at the official club in St. Petersburg.

It's a sturdy, powerfully built creature – males can weigh over ten kilos and females around six. It has a massive body with a solid bone structure, a very muscular back, shoulders and sides, and a broad, straight chest. Its legs are of medium-length; its large, slightly oval paws have little tufts of fur between the toes. Its tail is shorter than that of the Norwegian Forest Cat, but is strong and thick, covered in same-length hairs implanted perpendicularly from the base right to the rounded tip.

Its head forms a rounded triangle, with a wide forehead, high cheekbones and small, full cheeks. Its large, wide-open eyes are almond-shaped, set wide apart and slightly slanting. Its medium-sized ears are broad at the base, gently rounded towards the tips, with pretty wisps of long hair along the inner

RIGHT AND PAGE 202: Horacio des Loricaria of Siberia, "Agouti" and White Siberian Forest Cat, belonging to Mrs. Micheline Bancarel.

edges. They are set well to the sides of the head, and tilt slightly forward.

The double coat consists of a thick undercoat and a rougher, water-repellent top coat. It is particularly spectacular in winter, with its breeches and superb ruff, which starts at the cheeks and partly covers the front legs. All coat colours are allowed, with a preference for "agouti" (coats with alternating light and dark areas).

This cat is a good climber and hunter, but a calm and reserved household pet. Siberian peasants probably used it as a guard-cat, because it has a tendency to growl at the approach of strangers.

MAINE COON

The Maine Coon is a true American cat, which owes its name to its state of origin, and to the raccoon! According to legend, it is the result of matings between the little masked mammals and local cats running wild in the forests. More seriously, it no doubt resulted from spontaneous crossbreeding between local shorthaired farm cats, introduced by the first pioneers, and Angoras imported by New England sailors.

This hypothesis is the most likely, but as it is not proven, those who hanker after more romantic versions are free to believe the following story: Marie-Antoinette gave her Angora cats to the Marquis de Lafayette when he was leaving for the War of Independence, and when the Royal Cats arrived in the New World, they forgot their noble origins and mingled with the local population... Whatever the truth of its origins, the Maine Coon was a pioneer at American cat shows and was a great success at Madison Square Garden in 1895.

Its fortunes began to decline in the early 1900s however, with the arrival of more "exotic" cats like the Persian and the

Right and following double page: Rexotic Gary, Brown Classic Tabby Maine Coon, belonging to Mr. Denis Basile.

Siamese, and it was not until the 1950s that breeders renewed their interest in it and it returned to favour.

It is a sturdy, medium-to-large cat, with a long, rectangular body. Its well-proportioned legs are strong and muscular, and it has big round paws with tufts between the toes. Its head is large, with high cheekbones, a medium-long nose and a strong chin. Its eyes are set well apart, on a slight slant; they may be any colour. Its large, pointed ears are set high on its head and well-furnished inside. It has a long, luxuriant, plumed tail. Its silky fur falls smoothly, but is shorter and more close-lying on its head and shoulders; the fine undercoat is covered with a glossy, slightly oily, protective coat. As with the Norsk Skogkatt, all colours are permitted, except chocolate, lilac and Siamese Points.

RIGHT AND FOLLOWING DOUBLE PAGES: Hindi of Kamloof, Black Maine Coon, belonging to Mr. Gérard Beroud.

TURKISH CATS

The first specimens of Turkish Angora cats were taken to Italy in the seventeenth century by the explorer Pietro della Valle. This breed originated on the high plateaus of the Middle East, and owes its name to the city of Ankara (previously spelt Angora). It contributed greatly to the development of the Persian, but then began to die out, overshadowed by the greater popularity of its rival. It was even threatened by crossbreeding in its country of origin, and was saved just in time thanks to a breeding programme imposed on Ankara Zoo by the Turkish government. In 1959, it was rediscovered by a visiting American breeder.

The Turkish Angora is strong, solidly built but graceful, with long legs and small round paws with tufts between the toes. It has a triangular head, and large, pointed, high-set ears with pretty wisps of fur inside. Its eyes are almond-shaped and slightly slanting, and it has a medium-length nose without a stop. Its bushy tail is long and tapering, and must be carried low. Its semi-long coat is fine and silky, without an undercoat; the adult cat has a ruff.

RIGHT AND PAGE 217: Gaëtan le Fétiche des Loricaria, Cream and White Turkish Angora, belonging to Mrs. Micheline Bancarel.

The Turkish Van is very similar to the Turkish Angora. It also comes from a native Turkish population in the region of Lake Van, where it was discovered by British breeders in the 1960s. It is known as the "Swimming Cat" because of its fondness for water. Its body is pure white, but it is distinguished by the auburn colour of its forehead and the top of its head, and its tail is similarly coloured, with faint ring-markings. It has pale amber, pink-rimmed eyes; its nose leather, the insides of its ears and its pads are also pink. Breeders are working on fixing its marking, in a variety of colours.

Goufy de la Belle Blanche of de la Perle d'Antalya, Fany, Hendjyie (ABOVE),
Houchka de la Perle d'Antalya, Turkish Angoras, belonging to Mr. and
Mrs. Jean Bernel.

Preceding double page and above: Gulka de la Lucière and her kittens,
White and Auburn Turkish Van, belonging to Mrs. Maryse Mayoux.
Right: Hadjan de Capoutan-Lidj, White and Auburn Turkish Van,
belonging to Mrs. Maryse Mayoux.

RAGDOLL

The Ragdoll is a big strong cat, with semi-long fur, deep blue eyes, and the point markings of a Siamese. Sometimes it has white mitts like those of the Birman, and it can be bi-colour when all its paws are white and it has a white inverted 'V' on its forehead. It is called Ragdoll because it's a gentle giant, which relaxes so completely when it's held that it goes quite floppy! It is appreciated by the public for this "floppiness," which makes it exceptionally docile and cuddly, although it's a quality that varies from one Ragdoll to another. No serious scientific study to date has determined the reason for this, and although this feature is supposed to characterize the cat, it is not included in its current Standard of Points.

Legend has it that the first Ragdolls were born to a cat that had been hit by a car; they were floppy due to antenatal trauma and passed on their limpness to their own offspring. But this story is genetically impossible: trauma is not a transmittable gene. It is therefore more likely that the Ragdoll simply inherited this quality from the placid Persian and gentle Birman which contributed, along with the Siamese, to its creation.

RIGHT: Bag-of-Rags Melissa.
FOLLOWING DOUBLE PAGE: Pandapaws Eddie,
Ragdolls, belonging to Mrs. Vanna Maria Tatti.

Pandapaws Eddie, Jonathan de Cyanara, Ragdolls, belonging to
Mrs. Vanna Maria Tatti.

SACRED CAT OF BURMA

The Birman, or Sacred Cat of Burma, has a long, strong-boned body with short, powerful legs. The male is stockier than the female, but must not have the compact shape of a Persian. Its head is broad and round, with full cheeks, a strong chin, a medium-length nose and a gently curving forehead. Its ears are quite small and set at a slant. Its deep blue eyes are almost round. The coat is silky, without much undercoat; it is long on the back and sides, short on the legs and face, with a full ruff beginning at the cheeks. The chest and belly are a pale eggshell colour, the back is a golden fawn, and the coat has the Siamese pointed pattern, together with the characteristic "mitts" and "socks." The toes are a pure white colour that extends over the tops of the paws, but must not extend too far, or go up the sides of the legs. Ideally, the marking should be the same on all four paws; but the rear paws may have a larger white area than the fore paws, provided the markings on left and right legs are symmetrical.

RIGHT: Fol Amour.
FOLLOWING DOUBLE PAGE: Henessy de la Perle d'Or,
Seal Point Birmans, belonging to Mrs. Nicole Godier.

ABOVE: Gentiane de la Perle d'Or,
Blue Point Birman, belonging to Mrs. Nicole Godier.
RIGHT: Filibert, Seal and Blue Birman, belonging to Mrs. Pascale Richard.

Preceding double page: *Hermès de Song-Hio, Red Point Birman,*
belonging to Mrs. Brigitte Rozet.
Above and right: *Hirondelle, Seal Tortie Point Birman,*
belonging to Mrs. Brigitte Rozet.

BALINESE

The similarity of their colours makes it likely that Birmans,
Balinese and Siamese once had common ancestors in the
Far East. But whereas the sacred cat, with its snowy paws, small
ears and fairly heavy body, came from Burma in the early
1900s, the Balinese appeared unexpectedly in litters of ordinary
Siamese in the 1940s. Its consequent development was very
similar to that of the Somali, a mutant Abyssinian with semi-
long fur: initially it was excluded from reproduction because
of its "defective" fur, but ended up attracting attention to itself,
and having specific breeding programmes devoted to it, to
preserve its Siamese qualities: its elongated, angular body and
colourpointed coat pattern.

*RIGHT: Pride and Freesia Casa Decano of la Draiecour, Blue Tabby and Chocolate
Tabby Balinese, belonging to Mr. and Mrs. Serge Ferenczi.
FOLLOWING DOUBLE PAGE: Alegrias Casa Decano of la Draiecour and her kittens,
Blue Tabby Balinese, belonging to Mr. and Mrs. Serge Ferenczi.*

MANDARIN

The Balinese and the Mandarin have identical morphology, which is similar in every way to that of the Orientals and Siamese shown in detail in the next chapter. But although the Balinese, a long-haired Siamese breed "fixed" in the 1970s, has been internationally recognized for a decade, the long-haired Oriental is still being perfected by breeders.

Called Mandarins, the specimens which correspond to the desired standard are crossed with Balinese for the "long-hair" gene, with Orientals for their colour, or even with Siamese, to the annoyance of purists. These crossings usually result in mixed litters, with a hotch-potch of Balinese, Mandarins and surprise kittens. The kittens that do not conform to the standards of either breed are called "variants"; they still have a perfectly legitimate pedigree, as well as the required morphology. They have genes which are potentially useful to fix the new breed, and represent an inevitable transitional stage. Even if they cannot be shown, they are used for reproduction. One day there will be enough authentic Mandarins for them to be mated together without too great a risk of inbreeding, and the resulting kittens will all – or almost all – be Mandarins.

RIGHT AND FOLLOWING PAGES: Gatz'Arts de la Draiecour, Lavender Mackerel Tabby Mandarin, belonging to Mr. and Mrs. Serge Ferenczi.

SIAMESE AND ORIENTALS

SIAMESE AND ORIENTALS

The Siamese and Oriental are both elegant creatures with a hint of the "Pink Panther" in their profile – perhaps the famous figure was modelled after them! They are identical in shape, but form two groups according to colour.

Firstly, the Oriental's eyes are as invariably green as those of the Siamese are blue; secondly, the colour of the Oriental's coat – whatever it may be – is uniform over the body, whereas the Siamese has a different colour pattern, known as "points," on its face, legs, ears and tail.

There is one notable exception: should the Foreign White be considered an all-white Siamese, or is it a dissident blue-eyed Oriental?

Siamese and Orientals are medium-sized cats; their supple, muscular bodies are slim and angular, and they have long, slender legs with small oval paws. The tail is long and fine, tapering to a point. The slender neck carries a triangular head, which widens out in straight lines from the nose; this triangle is extended by the large, pointed ears, which are wide at the

PRECEDING PAGE: Amadeus of the Sweet Cats, Blue Siamese, belonging to Mrs. Jacqueline Pierre.
RIGHT: Zissi of Tontuta, Chocolate Point Siamese, belonging to Mr. Jean-Louis Nicolet.

base. A hollow-cheeked or "pinched" effect around the muzzle is not considered desirable. In profile, the long, straight nose continues the line of the slightly convex forehead without a break. The almond-shaped eyes are slightly slanting, in perfect harmony with the triangles formed by the nose, head and ears. If we look at cat magazines from the 1970s, we see that the Siamese used to be less "pointed" and angular than it is today, proving that taste in cats evolves too, and that aesthetic research plays an important part in the selection work done by breeders.

Zissi of Tontuta, Chocolate Point Siamese, belonging to Mr. Jean-Louis Nicolet.

ABOVE AND RIGHT: Gengis Khan du Domaine Sacré, Foreign White Siamese, belonging to Mrs. Christiane Merckx.

*ABOVE AND RIGHT: Amadeus of the Sweet Cats, Blue Siamese,
and Hugo de la Pergola, Seal Point Siamese,
belonging to Mrs. Jacqueline Pierre.*

Hugo de la Pergola, Seal Point Siamese, belonging to Mrs. Jacqueline Pierre.

Amadeus of the Sweet Cats, Blue Siamese, belonging to Mrs. Jacqueline Pierre.

ABOVE: Rokon of Off, Lilac Point Siamese, belonging to Mr. Jacky Letourneau.
RIGHT: Farouk de la Rouvière, Chocolate Tabby Siamese, belonging to
Mr. Louis Coste.

ABOVE AND RIGHT: H'Isis du Domaine Sacré, Seal Tortie Tabby Siamese,
belonging to Mrs. Christiane Merckx.

ABOVE AND RIGHT: Enki de l'Île des Ravageurs, Brown Spotted
Tabby Oriental, belonging to Mrs. Liliane Lesongeur.

Above and right: Gaodi de la Rouvière, Lavender Oriental, belonging to Mr. Louis Coste.

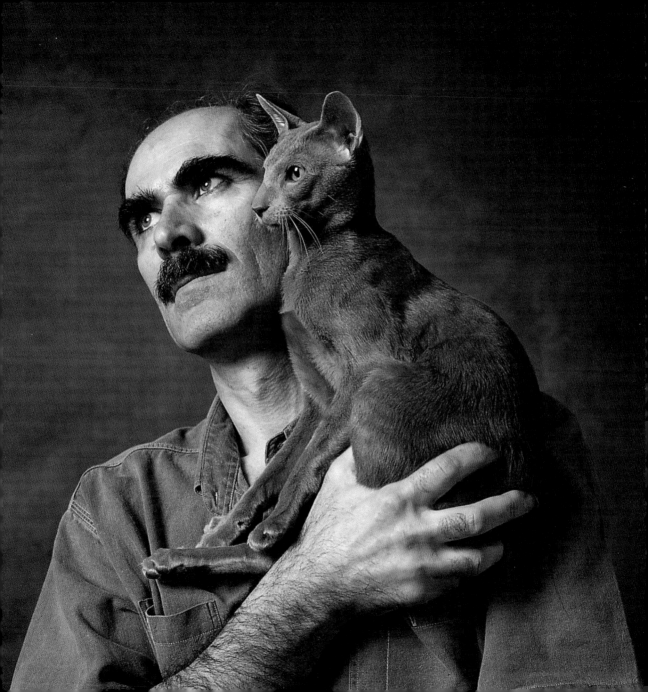

Above: Gavroche de la Clère, Chocolate Oriental, known as Havana, belonging to Mrs. Patrick Geslot.
Right: Hermès de la Malvoisine, Ebony Oriental, belonging to Mr. Alain Gilman.

Above, right and following double page: Gavroche de la Clère, Chocolate Oriental known as Havana, belonging to Mrs. Patrick Geslot.

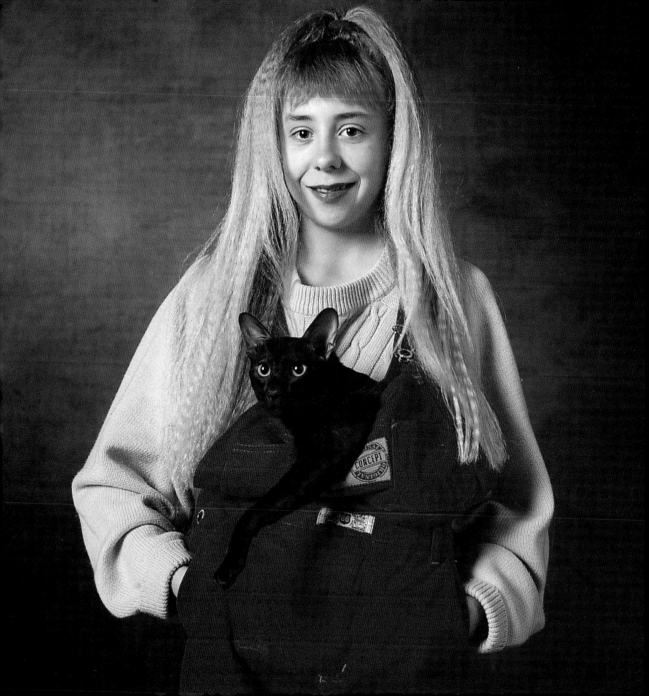

ABOVE AND RIGHT: Fifty-Fifty de Sophisticats, Bi-colour Black and White Oriental, belonging to Mrs. Chantal Dornat.

ABOVE AND RIGHT: Fifty-Fifty de Sophisticats, Bi-colour Black and White Oriental, belonging to Mrs. Chantal Dornat, and Hillou des Albatres, Cream Tabby Oriental, belonging to Ms. Élisabeth Contet.

ABOVE AND RIGHT: Dandy de la Romandière, Blue Tabby Oriental,
belonging to Ms. Élisabeth Contet.

*Above and right: Dandy de la Romandière, Blue Tabby Oriental,
and Harald des Albatres, Red Tabby Oriental.
Following double page: Harald des Albatres, Red Tabby Oriental,
belonging to Ms. Élisabeth Contet.*

PERSIANS AND EXOTICS

PERSIANS AND EXOTICS

Persian and Exotic Shorthair cats have the same "dense" morphology, and the same range of colourings. In both cases, the eyes, nose leather and pads must correspond to certain criteria, depending on the coat colour. The two breeds are differentiated by their type of fur: the Persian has a long, thick, silky coat, with a ruff falling over its chest and shoulders; the Exotic Shorthair is a shorthaired version of the Persian, with very thick fur which stands out from its body and is slightly longer than that of the British Shorthair.

Both breeds are medium-sized to large, with a massive body, broad chest, and muscular back and shoulders. The legs are short and thick, with large round paws, preferably with tufts between the toes. The tail is short, bushy in the case of the Persian, and must be proportionate to the body. The large, round face, lit up by big, round, pure-coloured eyes, gives these cats a moon-like appearance.

The ears are small, set wide apart and low on the head; they are slightly rounded, and well-furnished with fur inside.

PRECEDING PAGE: *Grain de Sable des Embruns, Cream Persian, belonging to Mrs. Bernadette Haule.*
RIGHT: *Gaspard de la Roizonne, Red Persian, belonging to Mrs. Élisabeth Kassis.*

The nose is small and short, without being turned-up, and there is a stop just between the eyes. The forehead is prominent, and the cheeks and chin are well-developed.

We can trace the origin of black or white longhaired cats called "Persians" back to the sixteenth century; the present-day Persian with its fantastic colours is a result of the work done by European and American breeders, who started developing it in the 1800s, using ever-stricter selection procedures to adapt its colours to changing tastes. The Exotic Shorthair, however – whose only exotic feature is its name – is a relatively recent cat. It did not acquire international recognition until 1984, but was created in the United States in the 1960s, from crossings between Persians and British or American shorthairs.

RIGHT: Geisha de la Lumière cendrée, Golden Shaded Persian, belonging to Mr. and Mrs. Robert Bonnin.

ABOVE: *Gaïa and Geisha de la Lumière cendrée, Golden Shaded Persians,*
belonging to Mr. and Mrs. Robert Bonnin.
RIGHT: *Lilian Buissant des Amorie, Chinchilla Persian, belonging to*
Mr. and Mrs. Robert Bonnin.

LEFT: Garfield del Adène, Red Tabby Persian, belonging to Mrs. Danielle Espiau.
ABOVE: Sweet Mary dell'Ariette du Shah-Li, Brown Tabby and Black Persian,
belonging to Mrs. Christiane Paillard.

ABOVE AND RIGHT: Hermione de la Brakelière, Blue-Cream and
White Van Persian, belonging to Mrs. Caroline Bonafos.

Left: Full-Ozass du clos de Bagneux, Persian, belonging to Mrs. Marie-José Tirard.
Above: Colombine de la Brakelière, Bi-colour Black and White Persian, belonging to Mrs. Yvette Framinet.

H'Ormacif and Full-Ozass du clos de Bagneux, Persians,
belonging to Mrs. Marie-José Tirard.

Stardust dell'Ariette du Shah-Li, Tortie Persian,
belonging to Mrs. Christiane Paillard.

PRECEDING DOUBLE PAGE: Geisha de la Brakelière, Harlequin Tortie and White Persian, belonging to Mrs. Nicolas Georgeault (RIGHT); Colombine de la Brakelière, Bi-colour Black and White Persian, belonging to Mrs. Yvette Framinet (LEFT).

LEFT: Hercule de la Brakelière, Black and White Van Persian, belonging to Mrs. Catherine Fromal.
ABOVE AND FOLLOWING DOUBLE PAGE: Gina de la Brakelière, Blue-Cream and White Persian, belonging to Mrs. Sylviane Bourgois.

*Above: Hercule de la Brakelière, Black and White Van Persian,
belonging to Mrs. Catherine Fromal.
Right: Fedora de la Brakelière, Tortie and White Persian, belonging
to Mrs. Sylviane Bourgois.*

ABOVE AND RIGHT: Harmonie de l'Arc-en-Ciel, Red and White Van Persian, belonging to Mrs. Catherine Fromal.

Above and right: Gamila de la Villouyère, known as Cannelle, Silver Tortie Tabby Persian, belonging to Mrs. Françoise Vigneron.

ABOVE AND LEFT: Eurydice Tresor de Bast, Colourpoint Persian,
belonging to Mrs. Dominique Guérinaud

Preceding double pages: Hermès de la Salamandre d'Or,
Colourpoint Red Point Persian, belonging to Mr. Robert Lubrano.
Above and right: Houpette et Geisha de la Charmeraie, White Persians,
belonging to Mrs. Lysiane Chavallard.

ABOVE AND RIGHT: Full-Ozass du clos de Bagneux, Red Shaded Cameo Persian, belonging to Mrs. Marie-José Tirard.

ABOVE AND LEFT: Follow Me Ice Cube, Colourpoint Red Point Persian,
belonging to Mr. Jean-Yves Ramel.

Above: Gigi du Chah Name, Black Persian, belonging to
Mrs. Élisabeth Kassis.
Right: Grain de Sable des Embruns, Cream Persian, belonging
to Mrs. Bernadette Haule.

*Preceding double page: De Gazeau's Gicolin, Tortie Smoke Persian,
belonging to Mrs. Brigitte Pottier.
Above and right: Élodée Magique des Lys Blancs, Silver Tortie Tabby Persian,
belonging to Mr. Christian Marechal and Mme Joëlle Riche.*

*PRECEDING DOUBLE PAGE AND RIGHT: Fall River des Lys Blancs,
Black Silver Mackerel Tabby Persian, belonging to Mr. Christian
Maréchal and Mrs. Joëlle Riche.
ABOVE: De Gazeau's Gicolin, Tortie Smoke Persian,
belonging to Mrs. Brigitte Pottier.*

ABOVE AND RIGHT: Daddy des Pujols of Royal Lys, Blue Silver Classic Tabby Persian, belonging to Mrs. Marie-France Dendauw.

ABOVE AND RIGHT: Doum-Doum du Pré du Curé, Blue-Cream Persian, belonging to Mrs. Nicole Richefort-Tsango.

ABOVE AND FOLLOWING DOUBLE PAGE: Grain de Sable des Embruns,
Cream Persian, belonging to Mrs. Bernadette Haule.
RIGHT: Geisha de la Lumière Cendrée, Golden Shaded Persian,
belonging to Mr. and Mrs. Robert Bonnin.

Above and right: Guizmo de Pomone, Colourpoint Persian,
belonging to Mr. Jean-Yves Ramel.
Following double page: Hursonne de Gremichka, Black Smoke Persian,
belonging to Mrs. Jeanine Perdriol.

*ABOVE AND RIGHT: Hursonne de Gremichka, Black Smoke Persian,
belonging to Mrs. Jeanine Perdriol.*

ABOVE AND RIGHT: Génaro de la Ronceraie Desravine, Blue Persian,
belonging to Mr. Gérard Beroud.

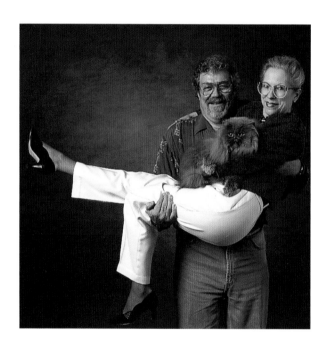

*Above: Foggy des Haudières, Blue Persian, belonging to Mrs. Catherine Fromal,
photographed with Mr. and Mrs. André Jocquel.
Right: Genaro de la Ronceraie Desravine, Blue Persian, belonging
to Mr. Gérard Beroud.*

ABOVE AND RIGHT: Trust of New World's Way Good-Love, Silver Tortie Tabby
Exotic Shorthair, belonging to Mr. and Mrs. Michel Sfez-Zon.

PRECEDING DOUBLE PAGE, ABOVE, RIGHT AND FOLLOWING DOUBLE PAGE:
Phalaenopsis Émile Victor, Red Tabby Exotic Shorthair,
belonging to Ms. Christelle Ponthieu and Mrs. Claudine Naels.

ABOVE: Hilary Tom Pouce Follow Me, Exotic Shorthair Creme Point,
belonging to Mr. Régis Machin.
RIGHT: Tasha Isatis of Follow Me, Blue Point Exotic Shorthair,
and Hilary Tom Pouce Follow Me, Cream Point Exotic Shorthair,
belonging to Mr. Régis Machin.

*ABOVE AND RIGHT: Hilary Tom Pouce of Follow Me, Cream Point
Exotic Shorthair, belonging to Mr. Régis Machin.*

Above and left: Tasha Isatis of Follow Me, Blue Point Exotic Shorthair, belonging to Mr. Régis Machin.

Preceding double page and right: Gitane nid'amour, Blue Silver Tabby Exotic Shorthair, belonging to Mr. and Mrs. Michel Sfez-Zon.
Above : Trust of New World's Way Good-Love, Silver Tortie Tabby Exotic Shorthair, belonging to Mr. and Mrs. Michel Sfez-Zon.

ABOVE AND RIGHT: Cake Bread Drambuie, Blue Mackerel Tabby
Exotic Shorthair, belonging to Mr. and Mrs. Michel Sfez-Zon,
photographed with Mr. Alain de Lavalade.

A LAST LOOK

"And specks of gold, like fine sand, are sprinkled like distant stars in their mystical eyes"

CHARLES BAUDELAIRE

What fascination there is in the cat's eyes, in that unblinking stare that draws and disturbs us, in those pupils that can narrow to a vertical slit or widen beyond measure to devour the coloured iris.

We feel an aesthetic satisfaction when we admire a cat, but to look into its eyes is an unsettling, even frightening experience. Even the most enthusiastic of cat-lovers feels a vague fear, mingled with respect. No doubt this disturbing sensation is due to some feline devilry ... if the eyes are the windows of the soul, the cat's eyes hold no comfort or reassurance for us, and its unflinching, undecipherable stare is devoid of all affection. And yet that unreadable eye is not empty – it seems to have access to an opaque and mysterious presence beyond. To look deep into the cat's eyes is to be aware of its absolute "otherness", and it requires great peace of mind to endure such a trial with equanimity.

When we look into the cat's eyes, we penetrate to the very heart of its "mystery" – if mystery it is. The puss that we scold for sharpening its claws on the sofa immediately assumes a suitably guilty expression, but there is not the slightest hint of remorse in its eyes. And when it abandons itself to our caress, we receive no loving looks in exchange – its whole body expresses its pleasure, but there is no change of expression in its half-closed eyes. It stretches out a furry paw, and spreads its toes in delight, demonstrating its feelings by gestures ... the literal meaning of the word "emotion", after all, is "outward movement". Whether it is hunting or killing its prey, lying in the sun or waiting for the magical fridge door to open at dinner-time, looking at a plate with thoughts of theft or grooming itself, the cat observes the world around it with its objective, unwavering eye. Only the angle of its head, ears and whiskers, and the tension in its neck, back and tail

RIGHT: Grisella Van Kievietsdel, Blue British, belonging to Mrs. Els Franssen.

betray the intensity of its concentration and its readiness to make a move. To understand a cat, one must learn its body language: like a perfect Zen soul, its eye is a non-reflecting mirror.

So is the cat Zen? According to a Buddhist legend, at the death of Buddha all the animals gathered, but only two remained dry-eyed: the cat and the snake. Along came a mouse, which began to lick the oil from a funeral lamp. The cat immediately pounced on it and gobbled it up.

Consequently, two schools of thought grew up regarding the creature: either it was an infamous, heartless beast that added insult to injury by committing murder, or else it was a wise animal, able to see through the illusory veil of sentiment and to react as the laws of nature dictate.

This legend once more demonstrates the cat's duality: angel if we love it and admire it for its "otherness"; devil if we hate it and find it disturbing. As for the cat itself, it still goes by its "wild lone", ears pricked and tail held high, while man theorizes to his heart's content and my own pussycat sleeps, curled up against the purring computer, pink nose on white paw, secure in the knowledge that she is The Cat, leaving us humans to ponder all the other questions.

Above: Hollywood Chewing Gum de Cour St-Éloi, Red and White American Curl, belonging to Ms. Florence Prescott.
Right: Petits de Gulka de la Lucière, White and Auburn Turkish Van, belonging to Mrs. Maryse Mayoux.

ABOVE: Hilary Tom Pouce Follow Me, Exotic Shorthair Creme Point,
belonging to Mr. Régis Machin.
RIGHT: Tasha Isatis of Follow Me, Blue Point Exotic Shorthair,
and Hilary Tom Pouce Follow Me, Cream Point Exotic Shorthair,
belonging to Mr. Régis Machin.

CONTENTS

INDEX

PRECEDING DOUBLE PAGE: Cats at the "Logis de Boncé" animal shelter, photographed with Mrs. Thérèse Arnac.
RIGHT: Héloïse de Cléomont, Smoky Black and White Cornish Rex, belonging to Mr. Jean-Pierre Filippi.